Teaching Healthy Cooking and Nutrition

in Primary Schools, Book 5

Chicken Curry, Macaroni Cheese, Spicy Meatballs and Other Recipes

Sandra Mulva...

D1338965

Brilliant
PUBLICATIONS

We hope you and your pupils enjoy trying out the recipes in this book and learning about healthy eating. Brilliant Publications publishes many other books to help primary school teachers. To find out more details on all of our titles, including those listed below, please log onto our website: www.brilliantpublications.co.uk.

Other titles in the Teaching Healthy Cooking and Nutrition in Primary Schools series:

Other titles published by Brilliant Publications

Published by Brilliant Publications
Unit 10,
Sparrow Hall Farm,
Edlesborough,
Dunstable,
Bedfordshire,
LU6 2ES

www.brilliantpublications.co.uk

The name Brilliant Publications
and the logo are registered trade marks.

Written by Sandra Mulvany
Illustrated by Kerry Ingham
Cover design by Brilliant Publications
Photography by Brilliant Publications
Printed in the UK

© 2008 Sandra Mulvany (text); Brilliant Publications
(photography, design and layout)

Printed ISBN 978-1-78317-112-5
e-book ISBN 978-1-78317-118-7

The first edition of this book, published in 2008, had the
title: Healthy Cooking for Primary Schools, Book 5.
This second edition was first printed and published in
the UK in 2014

10 9 8 7 6 5 4 3 2 1

The right of Sandra Mulvany to be identified as the
author of this work has been asserted by herself in
accordance with the Copyright, Design and Patents Act
1988.

Pages 7-89 may be photocopied by individual teachers
acting on behalf of the purchasing institution for
classroom use only, without permission from the
publisher or declaration to the Publishers Licensing
Society. The materials may not be reproduced in any
other form or for any other purpose without the prior
permission of the publisher.

Contents

Lesson	Recipe	Teaching	Learning Objective	
1	Pastry			13–18
	Croissant	Skill	How to Roll a Croissant	14
	Moons	Theory	Foods Contain More Than One Nutrient	15
		Health and Safety	Be Aware of Smells	15
2	Salmon Patties			19–24
		Skill	How to Coat Fish in Flour	20
		Theory	What is Omega 3 Good for?	21
		Health and Safety	Separate Cooked and Raw Meats	21
3	Chicken Curry			25–30
		Skill	How to Check Chicken is Cooked	26
		Theory	What is Salmonella?	27
		Health and Safety	Removing a Saucepan Lid Safely	27
4	Spring Rolls			31–36
		Skill	How to use Filo Pastry	32
		Theory	About Onions	33
		Health and Safety	Getting Rid of Waste	33
5	Börek			37–42
		Skill	How to Fold a Börek	38
		Theory	What is Feta Cheese?	39
		Health and Safety	Be Aware of Your Surroundings	39
6	Jambalaya			43–48
		Skill	How to Cut a Pepper	44
		Theory	Correct Food Storage is Important	45
		Health and Safety	Turn Handles Inwards Over Cooker	45

© Sandra Mulvany and Brilliant Publications

This page may be photocopied by the purchasing institution only.

Contents (cont.)

Introduction and Links to the National Curriculum

The *Teaching Healthy Cooking and Nutrition in Primary Schools* series is a practical school programme for schools. It focuses on the progression in cooking skills through easy-to-follow recipes. Essential cooking skills, theory and health and safety points are introduced progressively throughout the series.

The programme is designed to teach pupils practical cooking whilst incorporating the theory into the hands-on activity. Each of the five books in the series contains 12 recipes, together with visual lesson structure cards, visual learning objectives and photographs of the food – all of which are photocopiable.

All the recipes are presented in two formats, one laid out in a traditional way and one in a visual step-by-step format, enabling the recipes to be used with pupils of all ages or with groups with differing reading abilities. It is recommended that, after a cooking session, the recipes are photocopied and sent home with pupils, so that children can try making the recipes at home.

There are two assessment sheets in the book (on pages 85–86). The assessment sheets test and reinforce the practical and theoretical knowledge gained. You will also find a photocopiable certificate on page 87 for when pupils have completed all the tasks.

This second edition of *Teaching Healthy Cooking and Nutrition in Primary Schools* has been amended to ensure that it addresses the requirements of the National Curriculum for England (September 2014). The programmes of study state that pupils should be taught how to cook and apply the principles of nutrition and healthy eating. It aims to instil in pupils a love of cooking and to teach them a life skill that will enable pupils to feed themselves and others affordably and well, now and in later life.

Key Stage 1 pupils should be taught to use the basic principles of a healthy and varied diet to prepare dishes and understand where food comes from.

Key Stage 2 pupils should be taught to:
* understand and apply the principles of a healthy and varied diet
* prepare and cook a variety of predominantly savoury dishes using a range of cooking techniques
* understand seasonality, and know where and how a variety of ingredients are grown, reared, caught and processed.

The series also links well with the Health and Wellbeing section of the Scottish Curriculum for Excellence and the Guidance on the Schools (Health Promotion and Nutrition) (Scotland) Act 2007.

How to Use the Resources

All ingredients are based on two pupils sharing, and the timings will all fit into a double lesson of approximately 80 minutes. We recommend you use low-fat options where possible.

Make a display using the Visual Lesson Structure Cards (pages 7–10) and pictures of the recipe and skill to be focussed on in the lesson (colour versions of the photographs can be downloaded from the Brilliant Publications' website).

Keep the skill, theory and health and safety point sheets to hand so that you can refer to them when demonstrating to pupils. (The language has been kept as simple as possible on these sheets, so you may wish to give copies to your pupils as well.)

Choose the best format of the recipe to use for each pair of children and photocopy sufficient copies. The illustrated versions of the recipes can be photocopied onto either an A3 sheet (if space is an issue, fold it in half so that you view six steps at a time), or reduced to A4 size.

If you place the recipes and other sheets in clear plastic wallets (or laminate them), they can be used again and again.

Encourage children to gather together all the ingredients and equipment they need before starting. They could tick things off on their copy of the recipe.

Demonstrate the recipe 2–3 steps at a time, introducing the skill, theory and health and safety points as you progress through the recipe.

An important aspect of learning to cook is learning to work together. You may wish to display the Discussion cards on pages 11–12 (Communicate, Share, Help, Be pleasant) so that you can refer to these throughout the lesson.

The assessment sheets on pages 85 and 86 provide a fun way of testing the practical and theoretical knowledge gained. The Certificate of Achievement on page 87 can either be used as an ongoing record or be given out when all the recipes in the book have been completed.

On pages 88–89 there is a chart giving some suggestions for adapting the recipes for children with allergies and intolerances, and/or religious and lifestyle considerations. None of the recipes use nuts. Before you start any cooking activities, you should send home a letter asking parents to inform you if there are any allergy/lifestyle/religious considerations that you need to take into account. You may need to follow this up with a letter or phone call to clarify any issues raised. A useful chart listing some religious food customs can be found at: www.childrensfoodtrust.org.uk/assets/the-standards/3food-customs.pdf.

Above all, have fun and enjoy cooking!

Today We are Making

1

Today We are Learning

2

© Sandra Mulvany and Brilliant Publications
This page may be photocopied by the purchasing institution only.

Read Recipe

3

Healthy Cooking Recipe Book

Wash Hands and Prepare

4

© Sandra Mulvany and Brilliant Publications

This page may be photocopied by the purchasing institution only.

Cook

5

Clear Away

6

© Sandra Mulvany and Brilliant Publications

This page may be photocopied by the purchasing institution only.

Tasting

7

We Have Learnt

8

© Sandra Mulvany and Brilliant Publications

This page may be photocopied by the purchasing institution only.

Communicate

It is vital to have good communication in a cooking environment. If you are working with a partner, it is important to say what you are doing and to agree on who does what. You have to talk about what you would like to do and listen to what your partner wants to do. Then you have to work out a way to make it fair for both of you. You can only come to an agreement if you talk together!

You should also let others know if there are any dangers, such as you opening the oven or if water has been spilt on the floor. Talking is absolutely key to good cooking habits. The better you are at communicating, the better you are at cooking in a school environment.

Share

Good sharing follows on from good communicating. If you have communicated well, you will have reached a fair decision about sharing. Sharing works best when it has been done fairly and everyone is happy. Sharing is particularly difficult if it involves doing something really exciting or really boring. You have to imagine that the other person feels very much like yourself. This can be hard to imagine, but it is an important lesson to learn. Sharing is a lot easier when you talk together about things.

© Sandra Mulvany and Brilliant Publications

This page may be photocopied by the purchasing institution only.

Help

It is important to be able to help others, but it is also important to accept help from others. Help is a two-way thing. If you are offering your help to someone else, it is important that you choose your words carefully. Be kind in giving your help, as it can be hard to accept help given with harsh words. If you have communicated well, you will be able to help each other well. If you are very capable, offer your help kindly, but also let others help you in return, even if it is to do with something you feel you might already know about.

Be pleasant

It is, in fact, very simple to be pleasant. Look at and listen to the person you are working with and notice something he or she does well. Then say something pleasant about that. You will soon discover that the more pleasant you are to people, the more pleasant they are back to you. You can also do something pleasant, like smile at a person or pat someone kindly on the back. Don't just wait for someone to be pleasant to you; try to be the first one to say or do something pleasant.

© Sandra Mulvany and Brilliant Publications
This page may be photocopied by the purchasing institution only.

Pastry Croissant Moons

© Sandra Mulvany and Brilliant Publications

This page may be photocopied by the purchasing institution only.

How to Roll a Croissant

It is best to watch a demonstration of someone rolling a croissant. You will see that the dough is first rolled out into a circle and cut in quarters. Next, each quarter is rolled up, starting at the wide end and rolling into a point. Then the rolled-up dough is shaped into a crescent shape and the end or tip is tucked under the dough, so that it doesn't come undone during baking.

© Sandra Mulvany and Brilliant Publications
This page may be photocopied by the purchasing institution only.

Foods Contain More Than One Type of Nutrient

When we begin to learn about nutrients, we tend to generalize to make it simple. We might say that protein is found in meat and eggs, carbohydrates are found in bread and pasta and vitamins are found in vegetables. This is all true. However, most foods contain more than just one type of nutrient. When we say that eggs have protein in them, this is true, but they also have other nutrients in them, including vitamins A, D and E, B vitamins, iron and calcium. When we talk about nutrients in bread, don't forget that bread flour contains protein in addition to carbohydrates. On top of that, bread also contains yeast, margarine and sometimes milk, all of which have their own nutrients in them.

Be Aware of Smells

Always be aware of the smells in a kitchen, particularly when you have something in the oven. You can generally smell when the food in the oven is ready. You can also smell when it is burning. The more you bake, the more you will be able to understand the smells you smell.

Recipe

Pastry Croissant Moons

Ingredients: 100g wholemeal flour   25g plain flour
50g margarine   1 tsp baking powder   1 tsp cinnamon
1 egg   2 dsp milk

1. Put the oven on 200°C.

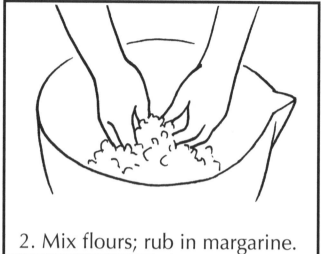

2. Mix flours; rub in margarine.

3. Add baking powder and cinnamon and mix it.

4. Crack the egg into a cup and whisk it.

5. Add the milk to the cup and whisk.

6. Pour the egg and milk mixture into the bowl. Mix to form a dough.

© Sandra Mulvany and Brilliant Publications
This page may be photocopied by the purchasing institution only.

Pastry Croissant Moons (cont.)

Equipment: Mixing bowl   Mixing spoon   Knife
Scales   Rolling pin   Baking tray   Measuring spoons
Cup   Whisk/fork   Flour dredger   Brush

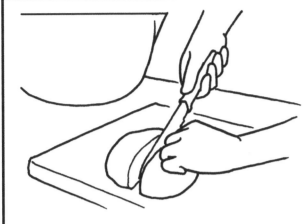

7. Divide the dough in two.

8. Roll each piece into a round shape.

9. Divide into 4 with a knife.

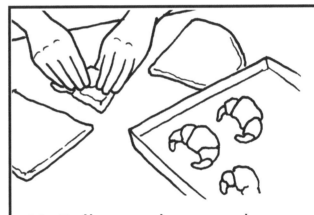

10. Roll up each part and put on a baking tray.

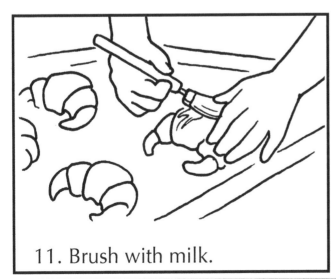

11. Brush with milk.

12. Bake in the oven for 10–15 minutes.

© Sandra Mulvany and Brilliant Publications
This page may be photocopied by the purchasing institution only.

Recipe

Pastry Croissant Moons

Ingredients:
100g wholemeal flour
25g plain flour
50g margarine
1 tsp baking powder
1 tsp cinnamon
1 egg
2 dsp milk

Equipment:
Mixing bowl
Mixing spoon
Knife
Scales
Rolling pin
Baking tray
Measuring spoons

Brush
Cup
Whisk/fork
Flour dredger

Instructions:

1. Put the oven on 200°C.

2. Mix flours; rub in margarine.

3. Add baking powder and cinnamon and mix it.

4. Crack the egg into a cup and whisk it.

5. Add the milk to the cup and whisk.

6. Pour the egg and milk mixture into the bowl. Mix to form a dough.

7. Divide the dough in two.

8. Roll each piece into a round shape.

9. Divide into 4 with a knife.

10. Roll up each part and put on a baking tray.

11. Brush with milk.

12. Bake in the oven for 10–15 minutes.

© Sandra Mulvany and Brilliant Publications
This page may be photocopied by the purchasing institution only.

Salmon Patties

© Sandra Mulvany and Brilliant Publications

This page may be photocopied by the purchasing institution only.

How to Coat Fish in Flour

Many fish recipes use breadcrumbs as a coating. Often you will be asked to coat the fish in egg first and then in breadcrumbs. Salmon patties are very moist from the outset, so we do not need to coat them in egg first. You can choose whether to coat the patties in breadcrumbs or just in plain flour. In either case, you put a little flour or breadcrumbs on a plate and then you simply turn the patty over in it several times to coat it. The flour will help to make the patty more solid and stick together better.

© Sandra Mulvany and Brilliant Publications

This page may be photocopied by the purchasing institution only.

What is Omega 3 Good for?

Omega 3 is found in all fish. The main source for omega 3 is found in oily fish such as tuna, sardines, salmon and mackerel, but is also present in soya, pumpkin seeds, walnuts and leafy-green vegetables in small quantities. Omega 3 is a type of fat, but it is a good fat which has many health benefits and therefore it is a fat we need a lot of. One major benefit is that it is very good for the heart. Scientific studies also point to the fact that Omega 3 is very good for the brain and helps to relieve anxiety, depression and ADHD. It is also a natural anti-inflammatory.

Separate Cooked and Raw Meats

Keep cooked food and raw meat separate.

This recipe calls for tinned salmon. However, you can also use fresh salmon, bought in most supermarkets. If you bought fresh salmon you would need to keep it separate from the cooked foods. We need to keep cooked food and raw meat separate. This is because the raw meat, and its juices can contaminate any cooked food. Always use separate equipment for raw meat and always keep raw meat separate from other food in the fridge, in your shopping trolley and in your shopping bags.

© Sandra Mulvany and Brilliant Publications

This page may be photocopied by the purchasing institution only.

Recipe

Salmon Patties

Ingredients:

1 tin of salmon	200g potatoes	2 tbsp chives
1 tsp plain flour	6 pitted black olives	1 egg
1 tbsp olive oil		

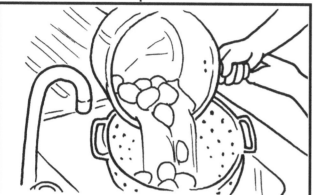

1. Boil the potatoes and drain when ready.

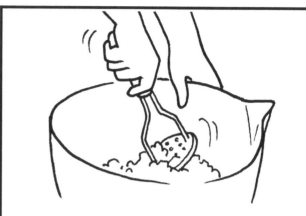

2. Mash potatoes in a bowl.

3. Crack an egg into a cup, whisk and add to bowl.

4. Add flour to bowl and mash.

5. Slice olives and mix into mixture.

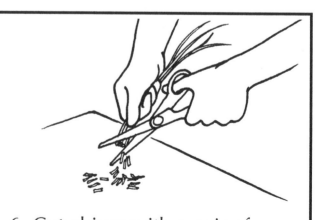

6. Cut chives with a pair of scissors and mix into mixture.

© Sandra Mulvany and Brilliant Publications
This page may be photocopied by the purchasing institution only.

Salmon Patties (cont.)

Equipment:

Saucepan	Plate	Colander	Frying pan	Sharp knife
Turner	Cup	Sieve	Potato masher	Whisk/fork	Teaspoon
Chopping board		Scissors	Mixing bowl	Tin opener

7. Open tin of salmon and drain in a sieve.

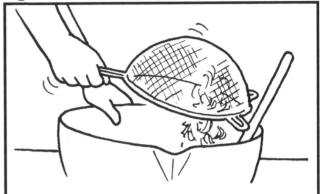

8. Mix salmon flakes into mixture.

9. Lightly flour your hands and form mixture into 4 patties.

10. Coat each patty in flour.

11. Heat olive oil in a frying pan.

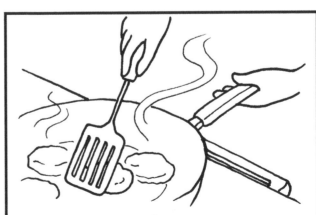

12. Fry patties for 3 minutes on each side or until golden.

© Sandra Mulvany and Brilliant Publications

This page may be photocopied by the purchasing institution only.

Teaching Healthy Cooking and Nutrition, Book 5

Recipe

Salmon Patties

Ingredients:
1 tin of salmon
200g potatoes
2 tbsp chives
6 pitted black olives
1 egg
1 tsp plain flour
1 tbsp olive oil

Equipment:
Saucepan   Potato masher
Plate   Whisk/fork
Colander   Teaspoon
Frying pan   Chopping board
Sharp knife   Scissors
Turner   Mixing bowl
Cup   Tin opener
Sieve

Instructions:

1.   Boil the potatoes and drain when ready.

2.   Mash potatoes in a bowl.

3.   Crack an egg into a cup, whisk and add to bowl.

4.   Add flour to bowl and mash.

5.   Slice olives and mix into mixture.

6.   Cut chives with a pair of scissors and mix into mixture.

7.   Open tin of salmon and drain in a sieve.

8.   Mix salmon flakes into mixture.

9.   Lightly flour your hands and form mixture into 4 patties.

10.   Coat each patty in flour.

11.   Heat olive oil in a frying pan.

12.   Fry patties for 3 minutes on each side or until golden.

© Sandra Mulvany and Brilliant Publications
This page may be photocopied by the purchasing institution only.

Chicken Curry

© Sandra Mulvany and Brilliant Publications
This page may be photocopied by the purchasing institution only.

Skill

How to Check Chicken is Cooked

To check whether your chicken pieces are done, you simply take a chicken piece out of the saucepan and cut it. The chicken is done if the centre is no longer pink. For chicken with bones in, you stick a fork or a knife into the meat; if the juices run clear, it is done.

© Sandra Mulvany and Brilliant Publications
This page may be photocopied by the purchasing institution only.

What is Salmonella?

Salmonella is a type of bacteria found particularly in chicken and eggs. The salmonella bacteria attack the stomach and intestines. If you get salmonella poisoning, you could suffer from diarrhoea, vomiting and fever. You can avoid salmonella infections by always washing your hands before preparing food and after touching meat, by observing good kitchen hygiene, by proper storage of food and by cooking food (particularly eggs and chicken) thoroughly.

Removing a Saucepan Lid Safely

If you have a lid on your saucepan, you must be careful when you lift it off. This is because the steam inside the saucepan will escape rapidly and can burn you. Therefore, when you take off the lid, stand well clear and turn the lid slightly to allow the steam to be released without any obstructions. This will also allow any water to drain off.

© Sandra Mulvany and Brilliant Publications

This page may be photocopied by the purchasing institution only.

Teaching Healthy Cooking and Nutrition, Book 5

www.brilliantpublications.co.uk   **27**

Chicken Curry

Ingredients:

1 chicken breast   1 onion   1 stock cube   1 apple
1 clove of garlic   2 tsp curry powder   Water
Small handful sultanas   Oil

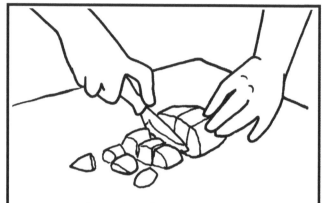

1. Cut the chicken into cubes. Wash your hands.

2. On another chopping board, peel and chop the onion.

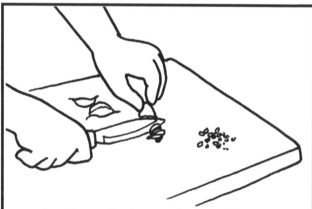

3. Peel and chop the garlic finely.

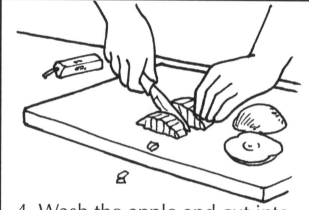

4. Wash the apple and cut into small pieces.

5. Heat a little oil in a saucepan.

6. Fry the chicken and onion.

© Sandra Mulvany and Brilliant Publications
This page may be photocopied by the purchasing institution only.

Chicken Curry (cont.)

Recipe

Equipment:

2 chopping boards | 2 sharp knives | Saucepan
Mixing spoon | Teaspoon | Measuring jug

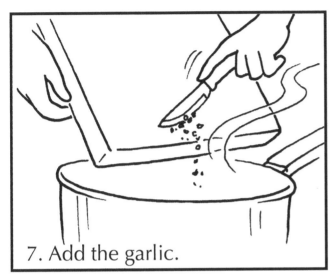

7. Add the garlic.

8. Add the curry powder and mix.

9. Add the apples and sultanas.

10. Add water to cover ingredients and add stock cube.

11. Put lid on and simmer for 15–20 minutes.

12. Serve with rice.

© Sandra Mulvany and Brilliant Publications
This page may be photocopied by the purchasing institution only.

Skill

Chicken Curry

Ingredients:
1 chicken breast
1 onion
1 stock cube
1 apple
1 clove of garlic
Water
Small handful sultanas
2 tsp curry powder
Oil

Equipment:
2 chopping boards
2 sharp knives
Saucepan
Mixing spoon
Teaspoon
Measuring jug

Instructions:

1.   Cut the chicken into cubes. Wash your hands.

2.   On another chopping board, peel and chop the onion.

3.   Peel and chop the garlic finely.

4.   Wash the apple and cut into small pieces.

5.   Heat a little oil in a saucepan.

6.   Fry the chicken and onion.

7.   Add the garlic.

8.   Add the curry powder and mix.

9.   Add the apple and sultanas.

10.   Add water to cover ingredients and add stock cube.

11.   Put lid on and simmer for 15–20 minutes.

12.   Serve with rice.

© Sandra Mulvany and Brilliant Publications
This page may be photocopied by the purchasing institution only.

Spring Rolls

© Sandra Mulvany and Brilliant Publications

This page may be photocopied by the purchasing institution only.

How to Use Filo Pastry

Filo pastry consists of paper-thin dough. When you use it, you have to be both careful and quick. Filo pastry tears easily and it dries out very quickly as well, especially in a hot kitchen. As soon as you have taken the filo pastry you need, cover the rest up in cling film again.

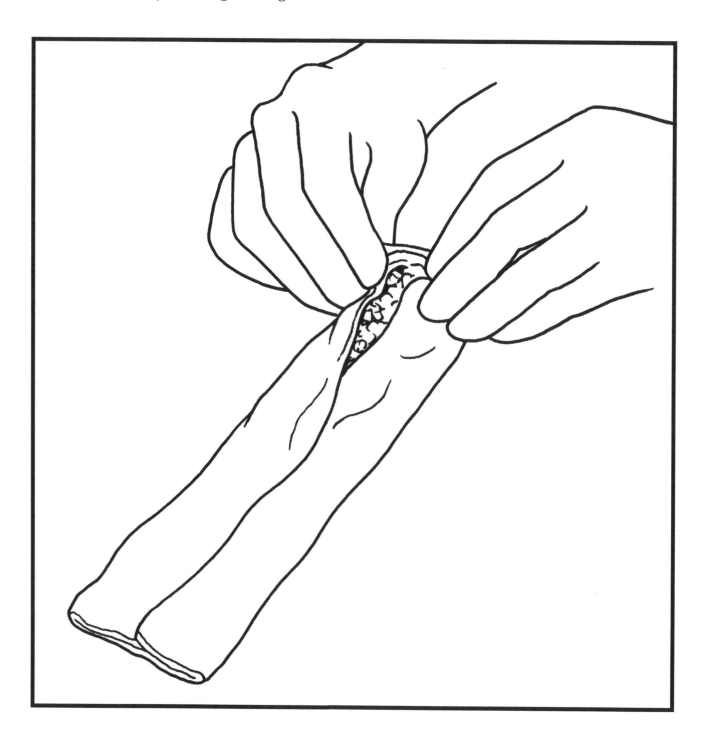

© Sandra Mulvany and Brilliant Publications
This page may be photocopied by the purchasing institution only.

About Onions

Onions come in a wide range of sizes, shapes and colours, as well as specific varieties. There are fresh onions and onions for storage. There are onions for eating raw and onions for cooking. Basically there are three kinds of onions: *bunching* onions which include spring onions and green onions; *bulb or common* onions including dry onions for storing or for cooking; and *pickling* onions.

Onions were important in the religious beliefs of the ancient Egyptians. This was because they thought the onion's round shape and concentric rings symbolized eternal life. As with any other circle or ring, there is no beginning and no end; it simply goes round endlessly. The ancient Egyptians even buried their dead with onions. Ramesses IV was buried with onion rings placed on his eyes. It was believed that the strong smell of the onions would bring back breath to the dead.

Getting Rid of Waste

You should always keep your kitchen bin clean. This is because it is an environment where micro-organisms will thrive. Always have a lid on the bin and keep it closed. When you remove the bin bag, tie a knot in it and put it straight in your outdoor bin. Your outdoor bin should be well away from the kitchen and should always have the lid closed. Some people recycle their organic waste for compost. This must also be done in a hygienic way, using a bin with a lid and regularly emptying and cleaning the bin.

© Sandra Mulvany and Brilliant Publications
This page may be photocopied by the purchasing institution only.

Spring Rolls

Ingredients:

3 sheets of filo pastry (24cm x 40cm)   50g carrot
50g courgette   2 spring onions   50g bean sprouts
Pinch of ginger   Olive oil

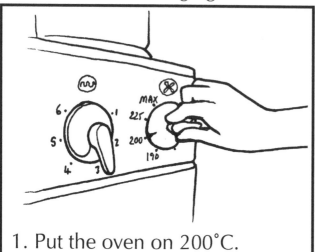

1. Put the oven on 200°C.

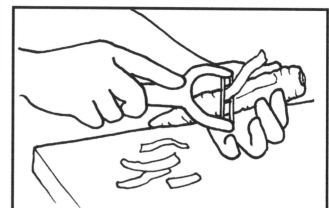

2. Peel and grate the carrot and put in bowl.

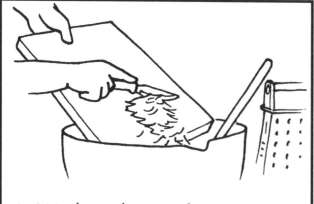

3. Wash and grate the courgette and put in bowl.

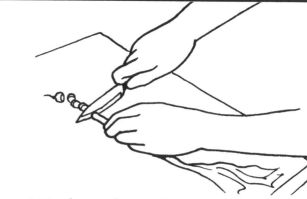

4. Wash and cut the spring onions and put in bowl.

5. Add bean sprouts and mix.

6. Add ginger and mix.

© Sandra Mulvany and Brilliant Publications
This page may be photocopied by the purchasing institution only.

Spring Rolls (cont.)

Recipe

Equipment:
Peeler   Knife   Grater   Brush   Sharp knife

Chopping board   Baking tray   Baking paper   Mixing bowl

Mixing spoon   Scales   Teaspoon

7. Put filo pastry on table, cut in half lengthwise and brush with olive oil.

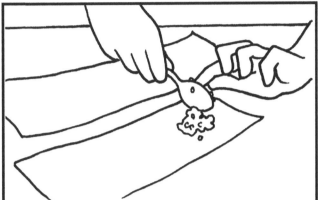

8. Put some mixture at one end, leaving edges free.

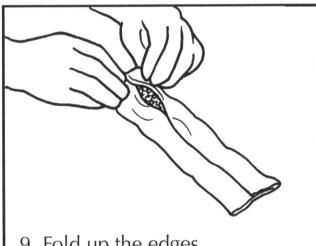

9. Fold up the edges.

10. Roll up the spring roll and brush with olive oil.

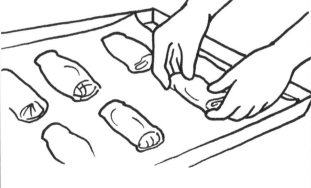

11. Put on baking paper on baking tray. Repeat with rest.

12. Bake for 10 minutes.

© Sandra Mulvany and Brilliant Publications

This page may be photocopied by the purchasing institution only.

Teaching Healthy Cooking and Nutrition, Book 5

Recipe

Spring Rolls

Ingredients:
3 sheets of filo pastry (24cm x 40cm)
50g courgette
50g carrot
2 spring onions
50g bean sprouts
Pinch of ginger
Olive oil

Equipment:
Peeler
Knife
Grater
Brush
Sharp knife
Chopping board
Baking tray
Baking paper
Mixing bowl
Mixing spoon
Scales
Teaspoon

Instructions:

1.   Put the oven on 200°C.

2.   Peel and grate the carrot and put in bowl.

3.   Wash and grate the courgette and put in bowl.

4.   Wash and cut the spring onions and put in bowl.

5.   Add bean sprouts and mix.

6.   Add ginger and mix.

7.   Put filo pastry on table, cut in half lengthwise and brush with olive oil.

8.   Put some mixture at one end, leaving edges free.

9.   Fold up the edges.

10.   Roll up the spring roll and brush with olive oil.

11.   Put on baking paper on baking tray. Repeat with rest.

12.   Bake for 10 minutes.

© Sandra Mulvany and Brilliant Publications
This page may be photocopied by the purchasing institution only.

Börek

© Sandra Mulvany and Brilliant Publications

This page may be photocopied by the purchasing institution only.

How to Fold a Börek

Börek is a pastry dish originating from Turkey and the Middle East. They are usually filled with cheese, potato, spinach or ground lamb and are often folded in the same way as a samosa. You take the filo pastry and cut it in half lengthwise. When you have brushed the strips with oil, you put a teaspoon of the mixture in the corner. Then you start folding the pastry into triangles. Watch a demonstration of it and then try to do it yourself.

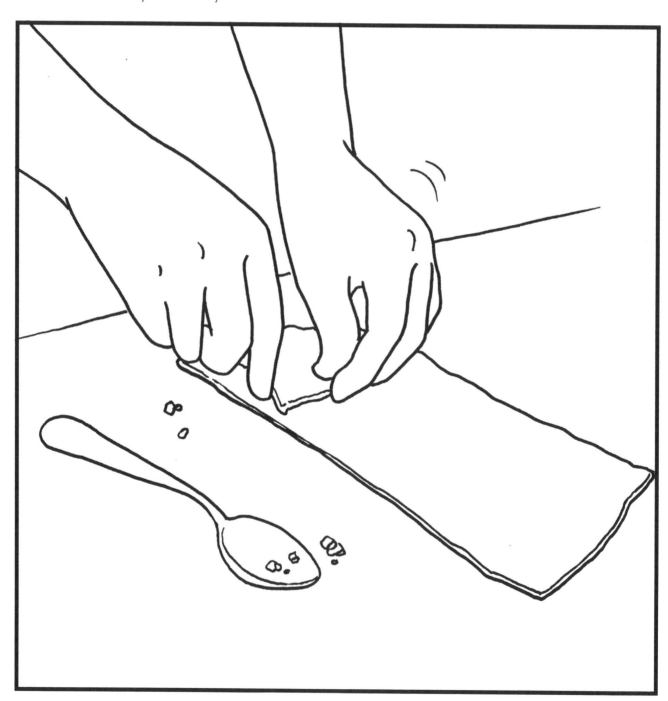

© Sandra Mulvany and Brilliant Publications
This page may be photocopied by the purchasing institution only.

What is Feta Cheese?

Feta cheese comes from Greek cuisine. It is a cheese that is salted and cured in brine for several months. Brine is salty water. Traditionally, feta cheese is made from goat's milk or sheep's milk. It is mainly produced in blocks and has a grainy texture. Feta cheese is a soft white cheese which has a rich tangy salty flavour.

Feta can be crumbled over salads (the Classic Greek Salad), or mixed together with sliced tomatoes, sprinkled with olive oil and fresh herbs. It is also used as a filling for puff pastry.

Be Aware of Your Surroundings

Make sure you have a general feeling/awareness of what is going on around you in the cooking area. Don't just concente on one detail of the recipe at a time, know what the next step is going to be and be aware of the other people around you and what stages they have reached. Make sure you keep the cooking area clean and tidy as you go, as this minimises the risks of accidents. The more time you spend working in the cooking area, the more aware you will become of the complete process and the easier it will get.

Recipe

Börek

Ingredients:
125g filo pastry	2 tbsp olive oil	150g feta cheese
Fresh mint	Pinch of pepper	Pinch of nutmeg

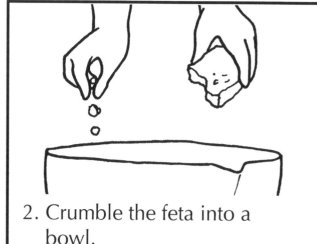

1. Put the oven on 180°C.

2. Crumble the feta into a bowl.

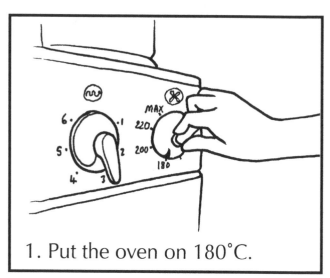

3. Add nutmeg and pepper and mix.

4. Wash the mint and cut up with scissors.

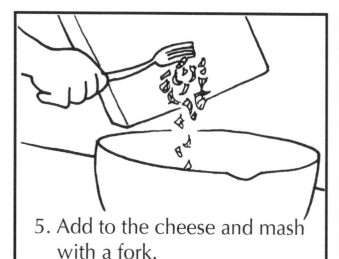

5. Add to the cheese and mash with a fork.

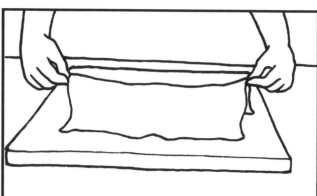

6. Place the filo pastry on the work surface.

© Sandra Mulvany and Brilliant Publications

This page may be photocopied by the purchasing institution only.

Börek (cont.)

Equipment:

Mixing bowl	Baking tray	Mixing spoon	
Scales	Scissors	Fork	Baking paper
Knife	Brush	Teaspoon	

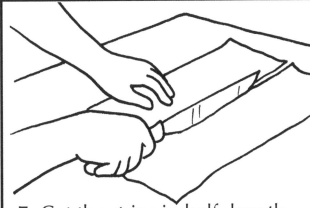

7. Cut the strips in half, length wise.

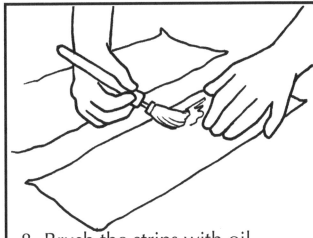

8. Brush the strips with oil.

9. Put a teaspoon of the mixture in the corner.

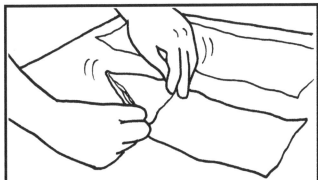

10. Fold the börek until you have a triangle. Repeat with rest of pastry.

11. Put on baking paper on baking tray and brush with oil.

12. Bake for 20 minutes.

© Sandra Mulvany and Brilliant Publications
This page may be photocopied by the purchasing institution only.

Recipe

Börek

Ingredients:
125g filo pastry
2 tbsp olive oil
150g feta cheese
Fresh mint
Pinch of pepper
Pinch of nutmeg

Equipment:
Mixing bowl
Baking tray
Mixing spoon   Baking paper
Scales   Knife
Scissors   Brush
Fork   Teaspoon

Instructions:

1.   Put the oven on 180°C.

2.   Crumble the feta into a bowl.

3.   Add nutmeg and pepper and mix.

4.   Wash the mint and cut up with scissors.

5.   Add to the cheese and mash with a fork.

6.   Place the filo pastry on the work surface.

7.   Cut the strips in half, lengthwise.

8.   Brush the strips with oil.

9.   Put a teaspoon of the mixture in the corner.

10. Fold the börek until you have a triangle. Repeat with the rest of the pastry.

11. Put on baking paper on baking tray and brush with oil.

12. Bake for 20 minutes.

© Sandra Mulvany and Brilliant Publications
This page may be photocopied by the purchasing institution only.

Jambalaya

© Sandra Mulvany and Brilliant Publications

This page may be photocopied by the purchasing institution only.

Skill

How to Cut a Pepper

The safest way to cut a pepper is to cut off all the sides. There are other ways of doing it, but this method is the safest. Hold the stalk of the pepper and use a sharp knife to cut down one side. Then put the cut side down on the chopping board and cut off the next side. Continue until you have cut off all four sides. You will be left with the core with all the seeds on.

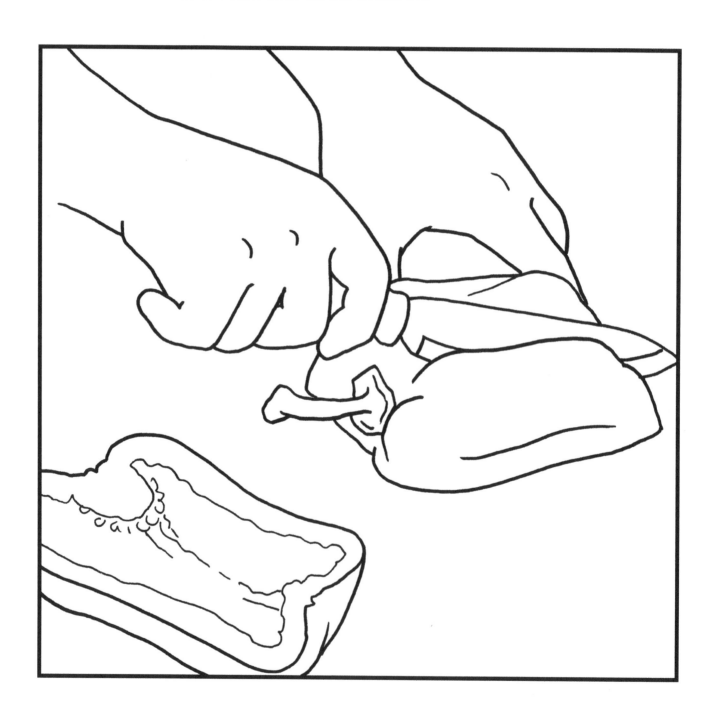

© Sandra Mulvany and Brilliant Publications

This page may be photocopied by the purchasing institution only.

Correct Food Storage is Important

Correct food storage plays an important role in maintaining good food hygiene. Some foods need to be stored in a cool and dark place, like a pantry. Other foods need to be frozen. Yet other foods need to be chilled in a fridge. Always make sure that you store food in the right place, at the right temperature and for the right amount of time. Remember that no food lasts for ever, however well it is stored. Check labels for storage instructions and learn where food should be stored.

Turn Handles Inwards Over Cooker

Always turn pan handles inwards over the cooker or work surface when using them.

When you are cooking foods in a frying pan or saucepan that has a handle, make sure that the handle never sticks out over the edge of the cooker. If the handle were to stick out, someone could easily walk into it by accident. This would probably knock the frying pan off the hob and onto the floor or even over somebody. Therefore, always make sure that the handle is turned in over the working area.

© Sandra Mulvany and Brilliant Publications

This page may be photocopied by the purchasing institution only.

Teaching Healthy Cooking and Nutrition, Book 5

www.brilliantpublications.co.uk   45

Recipe

Jambalaya

Ingredients:

1 sausage	1 onion	1 bay leaf	Water
Olive oil	1 pepper	1 stock cube	1 tomato	50g rice
1 stick celery	1 clove garlic		1 tsp Tabasco sauce

1. Cut the sausage. Wash your hands.

2. On another chopping board, chop the onion and garlic.

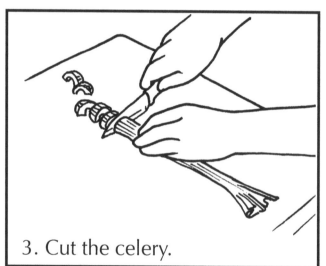

3. Cut the celery.

4. Chop the tomato.

5. Cut the pepper.

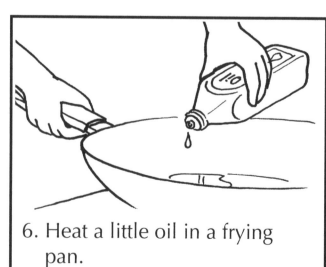

6. Heat a little oil in a frying pan.

© Sandra Mulvany and Brilliant Publications
This page may be photocopied by the purchasing institution only.

Jambalaya (cont.)

Recipe

Equipment:
2 chopping boards   Sharp knife   Frying pan
Turner   Teaspoon

7. Fry the onion and garlic and sausage.

8. Add the celery and pepper and fry.

9. Add the rice and fry.

10. Add bay leaf and water to cover.

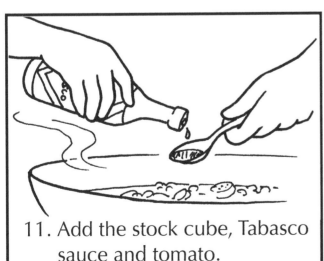

11. Add the stock cube, Tabasco sauce and tomato.

12. Simmer for 15–20 minutes.

© Sandra Mulvany and Brilliant Publications
This page may be photocopied by the purchasing institution only.

Jambalaya

Ingredients:

1 sausage   1 tomato
1 onion   50g rice
1 bay leaf   1 stick of celery
Water   1 clove of garlic
Olive oil   1 tsp Tabasco sauce
1 pepper
1 stock cube

Equipment:

Chopping board
Sharp knife
Frying pan
Turner
Teaspoon

Instructions:

1. Cut the sausage. Wash your hands.

2. On another chopping board, chop the onion and garlic.

3. Cut the celery.

4. Chop the tomato.

5. Cut the pepper.

6. Heat a little oil in a frying pan.

7. Fry the onion, garlic and sausage.

8. Add the celery and pepper and fry.

9. Add the rice and fry.

10. Add bay leaf and water to cover.

11. Add the stock cube, Tabasco sauce and tomato.

12. Simmer for 15–20 minutes.

© Sandra Mulvany and Brilliant Publications
This page may be photocopied by the purchasing institution only.

Bacon and Bean Pie

© Sandra Mulvany and Brilliant Publications

This page may be photocopied by the purchasing institution only.

How to Grill Bacon

There are many ways of cooking bacon: frying, microwaving, baking or grilling. To grill bacon, you simply cover the grill tray with tin foil and then place the bacon on (using tin foil will make the tray easier to clean). After this, put the grill on medium heat, and when it is up to temperature, slide the bacon under. Always keep an eye on it and turn it occasionally until it is ready. Be aware that hot fats can easily burn you and can catch fire quickly too.

© Sandra Mulvany and Brilliant Publications
This page may be photocopied by the purchasing institution only.

Where Does Bacon Come From?

Theory

Bacon comes from pigs. More accurately, it comes from the side, back or belly of the pig. Bacon can be cured or smoked, which means that the bacon is salted and dried or smoked. It is usually cut thinly into "rashers". Bacon is basically meat and fat; some bacon rashers have more fat on than others. You can see the fat, because it is white, so try to get the bacon with the least fat on it as it is healthier for you.

Shelf-life of Food

Health & Safety

Always check the sell-by-date and the use-by-date.

Always make sure that the food you are using has not exceeded its use-by date. This is easy on packaged products, as the sell-by date and/or use-by dates are displayed on the packaging itself. You should plan your shopping and cooking so that you can use the food well before its sell-by date. Also, check sell-by dates on the products when you buy them, and pick the freshest one.

Bacon and Bean Pie

Ingredients:

4 potatoes   2 rashers of lean bacon   25g cheddar

½ tin baked beans

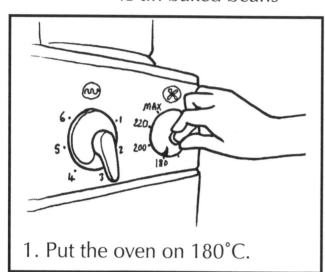

1. Put the oven on 180°C.

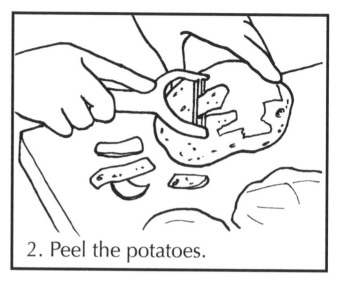

2. Peel the potatoes.

3. Cut the potatoes into chunks.

4. Boil the potatoes until ready.

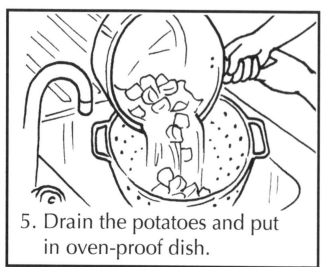

5. Drain the potatoes and put in oven-proof dish.

6. Grill potatoes for 5 minutes.

© Sandra Mulvany and Brilliant Publications

This page may be photocopied by the purchasing institution only.

Bacon and Bean Pie (cont.)

Recipe

Equipment: Peeler   Tin foil   Chopping board
Grater   Sharp knife   Mixing bowl   Mixing spoon
Saucepan   Colander   Tin opener   Oven-proof dish

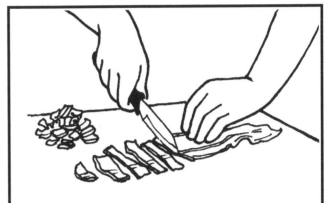

7. Put tin foil on grill tray and grill bacon.

8. Cut the bacon in small pieces and put in bowl.

9. Grate the cheese and add to bowl.

10. Add the baked beans to bowl and mix.

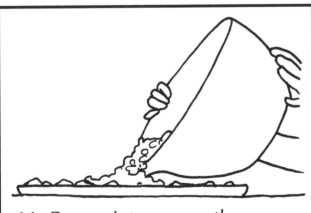

11. Pour mixture over the potatoes.

12. Bake for 15–20 minutes.

© Sandra Mulvany and Brilliant Publications
This page may be photocopied by the purchasing institution only.

Recipe

Bacon and Bean Pie

Ingredients:
4 potatoes
2 rashers of lean bacon
25g cheddar
½ tin baked beans

Equipment:
Peeler
Tin foil
Chopping board
Grater
Sharp knife
Mixing bowl
Saucepan
Mixing spoon
Colander
Tin opener
Oven-proof dish

Instructions:

1. Put the oven on 180°C.

2. Peel the potatoes.

3. Cut the potatoes into chunks.

4. Boil the potatoes until ready.

5. Drain the potatoes and put in oven-proof dish.

6. Grill potatoes for 5 minutes.

7. Put tin foil on grill tray and grill bacon.

8. Cut the bacon in small pieces and put in bowl.

9. Grate the cheese and add to bowl.

10. Add the baked beans to bowl and mix.

11. Pour mixture over the potatoes.

12. Bake for 15–20 minutes.

> **TIP**
> Share one tin of baked beans between two sets of partners.

© Sandra Mulvany and Brilliant Publications
This page may be photocopied by the purchasing institution only.

Wholemeal Drop Scones

How to Turn a Drop Scone

To turn a drop scone, you need to use a turner. Check that the scone is firm enough to flip over by peeping under it when lifting it slightly with the turner. When it is light brown, you push the turner under the entire drop scone and flip it over quickly, though not too quickly as you can splash yourself with hot oil.

© Sandra Mulvany and Brilliant Publications
This page may be photocopied by the purchasing institution only.

Testing the Freshness of an Egg

You can check the freshness of an egg by putting it in a bowl of cold water. If it floats, it has gone off; if it sits firmly on the bottom, it is fresh. If the egg is beginning to float, the freshness is somewhere in between. The floating happens because of the air pocket that is inside all eggs at the blunt end. As the egg gets older, the air pocket gets bigger, and this is what eventually makes the egg float. The air actually gets in gradually through the eggshell that is, in fact, slightly porous.

Hobs Remain Hot After Use

Pay attention when you are using the hob.

Always maintain a high level of awareness whilst in the cooking area. You should always remember to turn off the hob after use and remember that the hob whether it's gas or electric will remain very hot for a time while it goes through the cooling process. A great number of house fires are caused by carelessness in the kitchen; a deep-fat-fryer not being turned off after use will catch fire very quickly.

Wholemeal Drop Scones

Ingredients: 75g wholemeal flour   50g plain flour
½ egg   125g milk   1 dsp oil   25g caster sugar
Margarine   1 tsp baking powder

1. Sieve flours and baking powder into a bowl.

2. Add the sugar and mix.

3. Add the milk a little at a time.

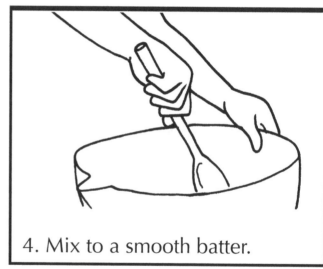

4. Mix to a smooth batter.

5. Add the oil and mix.

6. Crack the egg into a cup.

© Sandra Mulvany and Brilliant Publications
This page may be photocopied by the purchasing institution only.

Wholemeal Drop Scones (cont.)

Recipe

Equipment:

Mixing bowl	Sieve	Mixing spoon	Fork	Turner
Measuring jug	Cup	Frying pan	Scales	Measuring spoons

7. Whisk the egg with a fork.

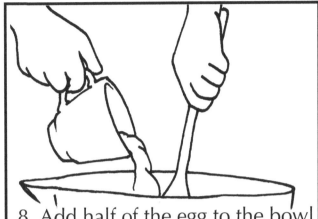

8. Add half of the egg to the bowl and mix.

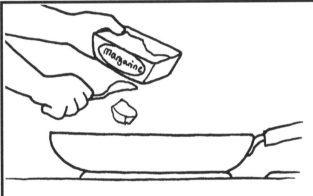

9. Put a little margarine in a frying pan and heat.

10. Drop a tablespoon of batter in the frying pan.

11. Fry until the tops bubble. Then turn.

12. Fry until all are done.

© Sandra Mulvany and Brilliant Publications
This page may be photocopied by the purchasing institution only.

Wholemeal Drop Scones

Ingredients:
75g wholemeal flour
50g plain flour
25g caster sugar
125g milk
½ egg
1 dsp oil
Margarine
1 tsp baking powder

Equipment:
Mixing bowl
Measuring spoons
Mixing spoon
Cup
Fork
Meauring jug
Sieve
Frying pan
Turner
Scales

Instructions:

1.   Sieve the flours and baking powder into a bowl.

2.   Add the sugar and mix.

3.   Add the milk a little at a time.

4.   Mix to a smooth batter.

5.   Add the oil and mix.

6.   Crack the egg into a cup.

7.   Whisk the egg with a fork.

8.   Add half of the egg to the bowl and mix.

9.   Put a little margarine in a frying pan and heat.

10. Drop a tablespoon of batter in the frying pan.

11. Fry until the tops bubble. Then turn.

12. Fry until all are done.

> **TIP**
> Share one egg between two sets of partners after you have whisked it.

© Sandra Mulvany and Brilliant Publications
This page may be photocopied by the purchasing institution only.

Tortilla

© Sandra Mulvany and Brilliant Publications

This page may be photocopied by the purchasing institution only.

How to Cook on Low Heat

It is a useful skill to be able to cook on a low heat. This means that you will have to watch the saucepan or frying pan closely and adjust the controls if needed. You also need to know what it looks, sounds and smells like when the food is getting too hot or even too cool. It takes practice to learn this properly. The reason for cooking food on a low heat is to cook it through thoroughly without burning it.

Teaching Healthy Cooking and Nutrition, Book 5   © Sandra Mulvany and Brilliant Publications

62   **www.brilliantpublications.co.uk**   This page may be photocopied by the purchasing institution only.

Tortilla is a Spanish Omelette

Theory

Tortilla is a Spanish omelette – very different from the thin, flat bread also called tortilla in Mexico. The Spanish tortilla is made with thin slices of potato and eggs. Other vegetables are often added as well.

Pathogens

Health & Safety

Bacteria are killed at 70°C.

Most pathogens (harmful bacteria) grow best in temperatures between 5°C and 63°C, with optimum growth around 37°C (the temperature of the human body). Pathogens are dormant at temperatures below 5°C. At temperatures above 63°C, their growth stops. However, pathogens are killed only at temperatures above 70°C. It is therefore recommended that to kill pathogens during the cooking process, food must reach a temperature of 70°C for 2 minutes. Therefore, make sure that your heat is not so low during the whole tortilla cooking process that it does not kill potential pathogens.

Tortilla

Recipe

Ingredients:

5 small new potatoes	1 small onion	3 eggs
1 red/orange pepper	5–10 runner beans	Olive oil

1. Wash the vegetables.

2. Cut the potatoes in thin slices.

3. Cut the pepper thinly.

4. Chop the onion in small pieces.

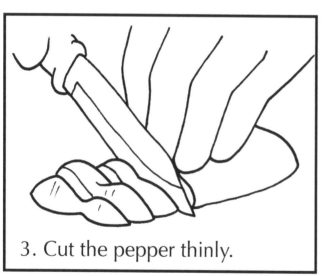

5. Cut the beans in small pieces.

6. Crack the eggs into a bowl and whisk.

© Sandra Mulvany and Brilliant Publications
This page may be photocopied by the purchasing institution only.

Tortilla (cont.)

Recipe

Equipment:
Chopping board   Sharp knife   Bowl   Whisk/fork
Frying pan   Turner

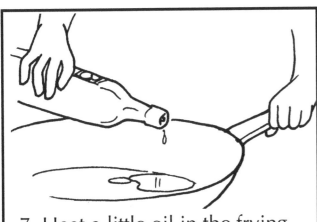

7. Heat a little oil in the frying pan.

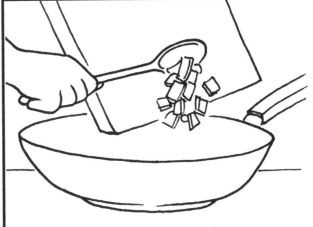

8. Fry the potatoes and onions.

9. Add the beans and pepper and fry until potatoes are done.

10. Pour the whisked eggs over.

11. Fry on a low heat until the omelette is golden brown on the bottom.

12. Put it under a hot grill to finish off the top.

© Sandra Mulvany and Brilliant Publications
This page may be photocopied by the purchasing institution only.

Recipe

Tortilla

Ingredients:
5 small new potatoes
1 small onion
1 red/orange pepper
5–10 runner beans
3 eggs
Olive oil

Equipment:
Chopping board
Sharp knife
Bowl
Whisk/fork
Frying pan
Turner

Instructions:

1.   Wash the vegetables.

2.   Cut the potatoes in thin slices.

3.   Cut the pepper thinly.

4.   Chop the onion in small pieces.

5.   Cut the beans in small pieces.

6.   Crack the eggs into a bowl and whisk.

7.   Heat a little oil in the frying pan.

8.   Fry the potatoes and onions.

9.   Add the beans and pepper and fry until potatoes are done.

10.   Pour the whisked eggs over.

11.   Fry on a low heat until the omelette is golden brown on the bottom.

12.   Put under a hot grill to finish off the top.

© Sandra Mulvany and Brilliant Publications
This page may be photocopied by the purchasing institution only.

Spicy Meatballs

© Sandra Mulvany and Brilliant Publications

This page may be photocopied by the purchasing institution only.

Skill

How to Chop Parsley

To chop parsley, you have to gather all the washed parsley leaves into a tight heap. Whilst you hold onto the heap with one hand, you chop it from one end. When it has been chopped roughly, you start cutting the heap of parsley again from one end to the other. If you are capable with a knife, you can guide the knife gently by putting your hand on top of the knife as you are cutting the parsley. Remember to gather the loose parsley every now and again and continue until all the parsley is finely chopped.

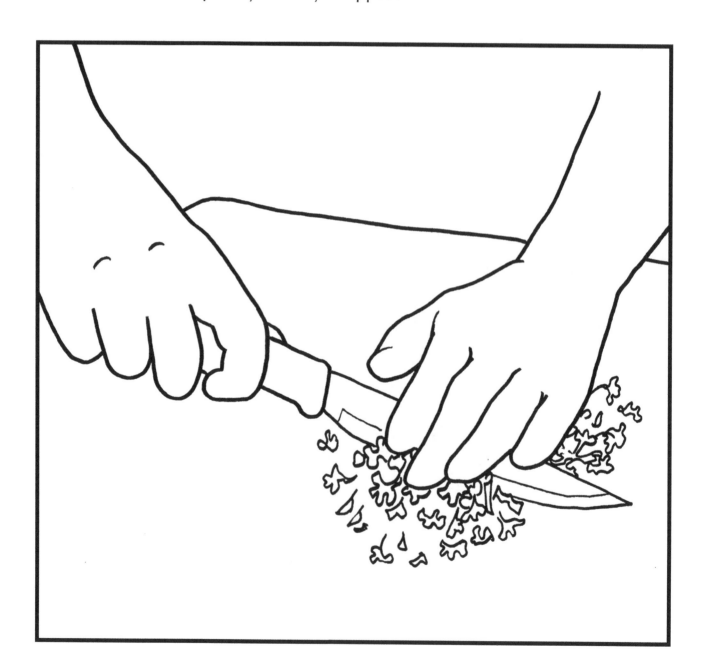

© Sandra Mulvany and Brilliant Publications
This page may be photocopied by the purchasing institution only.

How Do You Plan Your Meals?

When you plan your meals, you have to look at the bigger picture. The idea is that you get all the nutrients you need as often as you need. It is therefore sensible to plan a whole week's meals in one go, making sure that each meal covers all the basic nutrients. You do not need all nutrients every day, because the body can store certain nutrients, but make sure that these are covered some time in the week.

Storing Meat in the Fridge

Store raw meat at the bottom of the fridge.

Always store raw meat at the bottom of the fridge. This is to avoid cross-contamination, as raw meat may drip juices onto other food. Keep cooked and uncooked foods apart so that the uncooked foods do not pass on any bacteria to the cooked foods.

© Sandra Mulvany and Brilliant Publications

This page may be photocopied by the purchasing institution only.

Recipe

Spicy Meatballs

Ingredients: 250g lean sausage meat · 25g porridge oats
1 small onion · 1 tbsp tomato ketchup · 1 tsp curry powder
2 tbsp chopped parsley · ½ tbsp Worcestershire sauce

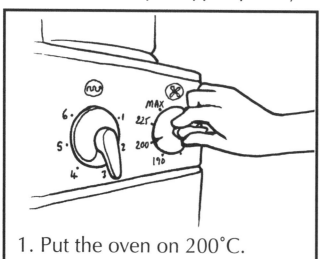

1. Put the oven on 200°C.

2. Chop the onion finely and put in bowl.

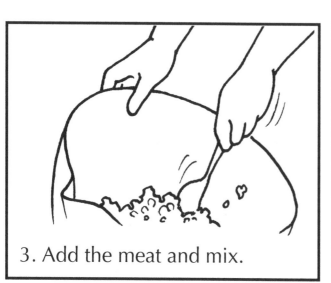

3. Add the meat and mix.

4. Add the porridge oats and mix.

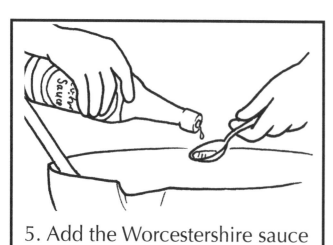

5. Add the Worcestershire sauce and mix.

6. Add the tomato ketchup and curry powder and mix.

© Sandra Mulvany and Brilliant Publications
This page may be photocopied by the purchasing institution only.

Spicy Meatballs (cont.)

Recipe

Equipment:

Chopping board	Sharp knife	Mixing bowl	Scales
Mixing spoon	Baking tray	Measuring spoons	

7. Wash and chop the parsley.

8. Add the chopped parsley and mix.

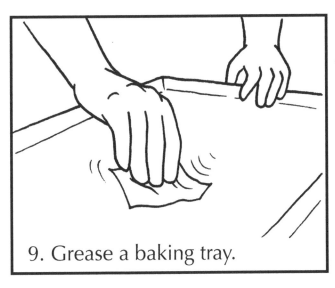

9. Grease a baking tray.

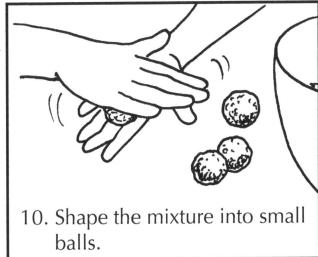

10. Shape the mixture into small balls.

11. Put the balls on the baking tray.

12. Bake for 25 minutes.

© Sandra Mulvany and Brilliant Publications

This page may be photocopied by the purchasing institution only.

Teaching Healthy Cooking and Nutrition, Book 5
www.brilliantpublications.co.uk

Spicy Meatballs

Ingredients:
1 small onion
250g lean sausage meat
25g porridge oats
½ tbsp Worcestershire sauce
1 tbsp tomato ketchup
1 tsp curry powder
2 tbsp chopped parsley

Equipment:
Chopping board
Sharp knife
Mixing bowl
Mixing spoon
Scales
Measuring spoons
Baking tray

Instructions:

1. Put the oven on 200°C.

2. Cut the onion finely and put in bowl.

3. Add the meat and mix.

4. Add the porridge oats and mix.

5. Add the Worcestershire sauce and mix.

6. Add the tomato ketchup and curry powder and mix.

7. Wash and chop the parsley.

8. Add the chopped parsley and mix.

9. Grease a baking tray.

10. Shape the mixture into small balls.

11. Put the balls on the baking tray.

12. Bake for 25 minutes.

© Sandra Mulvany and Brilliant Publications
This page may be photocopied by the purchasing institution only.

Macaroni Cheese

© Sandra Mulvany and Brilliant Publications

This page may be photocopied by the purchasing institution only.

How to Add Liquid Gradually

When you make macaroni cheese, you have to add the milk gradually to make the sauce. This enables you to mix a smooth sauce, and it allows the mixture to thicken slowly. You have to know how much milk to add, and you have to remember that it thickens gradually over heat and not straight away.

© Sandra Mulvany and Brilliant Publications

This page may be photocopied by the purchasing institution only.

How to Store Milk

You store milk in the fridge. Keep the milk container closed in order to avoid the absorption of other food flavours. Always return the milk to the fridge as soon as you have used it; don't just leave it on the table. Always use the milk before the best-before date.

Avoiding Obesity

Obesity is the terminology used to describe the condition of people who are very, very fat – more than just a few pounds overweight. It is, in fact, a medical term used for very overweight people (people who carry more than 20% extra body weight). These people are at an increased risk of a lot of diseases, such as diabetes, high blood pressure and heart disease.

To avoid obesity, you have to eat a healthy and balanced diet. You can eat as much fresh fruit and vegetables as you like, but remember to avoid eating junk food and sweets more than once-a-week as these foods are full of fats, salts and sugars. Exercise plays a key role to keeping your weight down, although some overweight people have medical conditions that prevent them from losing weight.

Eat sensibly, exercise more.

Macaroni Cheese

Ingredients:

150g macaroni   50g plain flour   250ml milk
50g margarine   50g cheese   Water

1. Put plenty of water in a sauce-pan and bring to the boil.

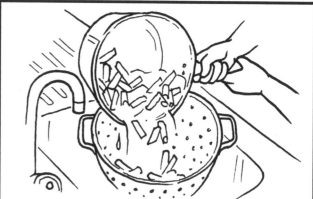

2. Boil the macaroni and drain when cooked.

3. Grate the cheese.

4. Measure flour.

5. Measure milk.

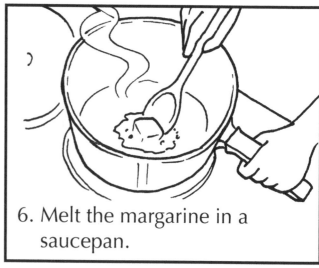

6. Melt the margarine in a saucepan.

© Sandra Mulvany and Brilliant Publications

This page may be photocopied by the purchasing institution only.

Macaroni Cheese (cont.)

Equipment:

2 saucepans   Colander   Oven-proof dish   Grater
Scales   Measuring jug   Mixing spoon

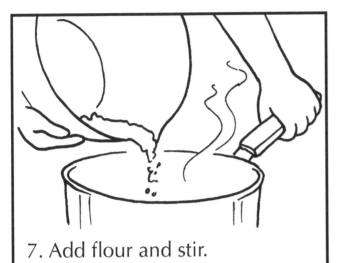

7. Add flour and stir.

8. Add a little milk and stir.

9. Add rest of milk a little at a time. Keep stirring.

10. Add cheese and mix.

11. Add sauce to macaroni and mix.

12. Put in oven-proof dish. Grill until brown.

© Sandra Mulvany and Brilliant Publications
This page may be photocopied by the purchasing institution only.

Recipe

Macaroni Cheese

Ingredients:
150g macaroni
50g plain flour
250ml milk
50g margarine
50g cheese

Equipment:
2 saucepans
Colander
Grater
Oven-proof dish
Scales
Measuring jug
Mixing spoon

Instructions:

1.   Put plenty of water in a saucepan and bring to the boil.

2.   Boil the macaroni and drain when cooked.

3.   Grate the cheese.

4.   Measure flour.

5.   Measure milk.

6.   Melt the margarine in a saucepan.

7.   Add flour and stir.

8.   Add a little milk and stir.

9.   Add rest of milk a little at a time. Keep stirring.

10.   Add cheese and mix.

11.   Add sauce to macaroni and mix.

12.   Put in oven-proof dish. Grill until brown.

© Sandra Mulvany and Brilliant Publications
This page may be photocopied by the purchasing institution only.

Vegetable Samosas

© Sandra Mulvany and Brilliant Publications

This page may be photocopied by the purchasing institution only.

Skill

How to Add Food Gradually

When you have a number of foods to fry in the same frying pan, chances are that you will not add them all at the same time. This is because different foods need different amounts of frying time. Some need more and some need less, and you add them gradually so that it will all be finished and ready at the same time. It takes a lot of food knowledge to be able to do this well.

© Sandra Mulvany and Brilliant Publications
This page may be photocopied by the purchasing institution only.

Where Do Samosas Come From?

Samosas are very common in South Asian countries, such as Pakistan, India and Nepal. It is believed that samosas originally came from Central Asia as far back as before the 10th century. Look for these places on a globe or a map of the world.

Traditionally, samosas are fried, but many people prefer to bake them nowadays.

A Healthy Mind in a Healthy Body

"A healthy mind in a healthy body" is in fact a quote from the Roman poet Juvenal (55AD to 127AD). It is a quote that has been much used ever since. Basically, it means that if you feel well physically, you will feel well mentally. Your mental and physical well-being are linked. We still very much believe this today when we talk about Healthy Living. In other words: exercise, healthy eating and happiness in general are all linked. Think about it!

Recipe

Vegetable Samosas

Ingredients: 4 tbsp oil   50g frozen peas   1 onion
Filo pastry   1 potato   2 carrots   Water
2 tsp garam masala   3 cauliflower florets

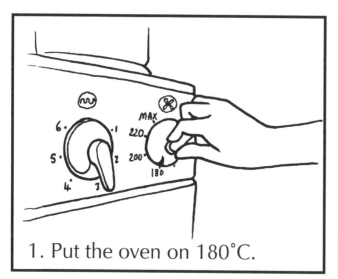

1. Put the oven on 180°C.

2. Peel onion and chop finely.

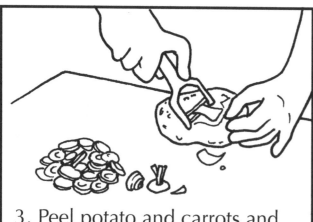

3. Peel potato and carrots and chop finely.

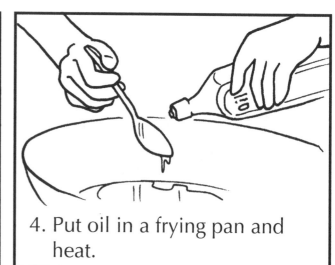

4. Put oil in a frying pan and heat.

5. Add onion and fry for 2 minutes.

6. Add potato and carrots and fry for 5 minutes.

© Sandra Mulvany and Brilliant Publications
This page may be photocopied by the purchasing institution only.

Vegetable Samosas (cont.)

Equipment:
Sharp knife   Baking tray   Chopping board   Peeler
Frying pan   Turner   Teaspoon   Tablespoon   Scales

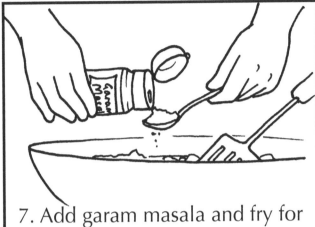

7. Add garam masala and fry for 2 minutes.

8. Add cauliflower florets.

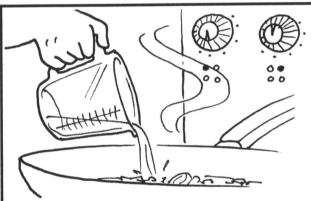

9. Add some water and simmer for 10 minutes.

10. Add peas and simmer until the water is gone.

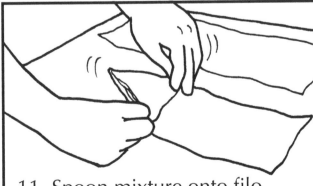

11. Spoon mixture onto filo pastry and fold samosas (see Börek, Lesson 5).

12. Bake for 10 minutes.

© Sandra Mulvany and Brilliant Publications
This page may be photocopied by the purchasing institution only.

Vegetable Samosas

Ingredients:
4 tbsp oil
50g frozen peas
1 onion
Filo pastry
1 potato
2 carrots
2 tsp garam masala
Water
3 cauliflower florets

Equipment:
Sharp knife
Baking tray
Chopping board
Peeler
Frying pan
Turner
Teaspoon
Tablespoon
Scales

Instructions:

1.   Put oven on 180°C.

2.   Peel onion and chop finely.

3.   Peel potato and carrots and chop finely.

4.   Put oil in a frying pan and heat.

5.   Add onion and fry for 2 minutes.

6.   Add potato and carrot and fry for 5 minutes.

7.   Add garam masala and fry for 2 minutes.

8.   Add cauliflower florets.

9.   Add some water and simmer for 10 minutes.

10.   Add peas and simmer until the water is gone.

11.   Spoon mixture onto filo pastry and fold samosas (see Börek, Lesson 5).

12.   Bake for 10 minutes.

© Sandra Mulvany and Brilliant Publications
This page may be photocopied by the purchasing institution only.

What Can You Remember? (1)

Take this quiz after lesson 6.

1. What could smells in a kitchen tell you?

   That food is burning   To change your socks   The dog needs a bath

2. What should you do after touching raw meat, poultry or fish?

   Sing Happy Birthday   Wash your hands   Wash the floor

3. What are bacteria that cause disease called?

   Bill and Ben   Cinderella   Pathogens

4. What colour should chicken no longer be when it is cooked?

   Blue   Pink   Black

5. Where is Salmonella found?

   In chicken and eggs   In flour   In baking powder

6. What did onions symbolize in ancient Egypt?

   Eternal sorrow   Eternal terror   Eternal life

7. What should you always have on your bin?

   A lid   A fairy queen   A pick-up truck

8. Where does feta cheese come from?

   Wales   Scotland   Greece

9. What type of pastry is Börek made with?

   Short crust   Puff pastry   Filo

10. Should frying pan handles stick out over the edge of the cooker?

   Yes, of course   No   Only on Sundays

Name _____ Date _____ Score _____

What Can You Remember? (2)

Take this quiz after lesson 12.

1. Where does bacon come from?

     Space   Pigs   Cows

2. If you put a fresh egg in a bowl of water, what should it do?

     Float   Explode   Sink

3. At what temperature are bacteria killed?

     30°C   40°C   70°C

4. How long should you cook bacteria at this temperature to kill them?

     2 minutes   1 minute   ½ minute

5. Between which temperatures do pathogens grow best?

     -5°C and 0°C   5°C and 63°C   100°C and 125°C

6. Where should you store raw meat in the fridge?

     At the bottom   At the top   In the middle

7. What should you keep cooked foods away from?

     Scary films   Uncooked foods   Bad company

8. What does "Obesity" mean?

     To be very overweight To be underweight   To be obedient

9. Where do samosas come from?

     Scotland   North Pole   South Asia

10. A healthy mind in a healthy … ?

     Body   Jar   Bottle

Name _____ Date _____ Score _____

© Sandra Mulvany and Brilliant Publications
This page may be photocopied by the purchasing institution only.

Certificate of Achievement

Teaching Healthy Cooking and Nutrition, Book 5

Name

_____

Is Able to

Roll a croissant

Coat in flour

Check chicken

Use filo pastry

Fold a Börek or samosa

Cut a pepper

Grill bacon

Turn a drop scone

Cook on low heat

Chop parsley

Add liquid gradually

Add food gradually

© Sandra Mulvany and Brilliant Publications
This page may be photocopied by the purchasing institution only.

Allergy/lifestyle/religious considerations

The chart below lists possible substitutions that can be made (where possible) for children with common allergies/intolerances and/or lifestyle/religious considerations. It is not exhaustive and it is important to check with parents prior to doing any cooking activities.

Recipe	Possible substitutions
Pastry Croissant Moons	This recipe is not suitable for children with gluten/wheat and/or egg allergies. (Alternative gluten free/egg free recipes can be found on the Internet.) Lactose free margarine and milk (eg oat or rice milk) may be used for children who are lactose intolerant.
Salmon Patties	Some vegetarians will eat fish, but others won't. Check with the parents.
Chicken Curry	This recipe is not suitable for vegetarians. Use gluten free stock cubes for any children with a gluten intolerance.
Spring Rolls	This recipe is not suitable for children with gluten/wheat allergies.
Börek	This recipe is not suitable for children with gluten/wheat allergies. Feta cheese is not lactose-free but it contains less lactose than other dairy products, so it may be OK for children with a lactose intolerance. Check with the parents.
Jambalaya	The sausage could be omitted for children who are vegetarians. For children who do not eat pork due to religious considerations, pork sausages could be substituted with turkey or beef sausages (but check that they don't have any pork in them). Use gluten free stock cubes for any children with a gluten intolerance.

© Sandra Mulvany and Brilliant Publications

Allergy/lifestyle/religious considerations (cont.)

Recipe	Possible substitutions
Bacon and Bean Pie	The bacon could be omitted for children who are vegetarians. It is not suitable for children who don't eat pork due to religious considerations. Check that the baked beans are gluten free, as some brands contain gluten. Lactose free hard cheese may be used for children who are lactose intolerant.
Wholemeal Drop Scones	This recipe is not suitable for children with gluten/wheat and/or egg allergies. Lactose free milk and margarine may be used for children who are lactose intolerant.
Tortilla	This recipe is not suitable for children will egg allergies.
Spicy meatballs	This recipe is not suitable for children who are vegetarians. Mince beef could be used instead of sausage meat, but the meatballs will not stick together as well. You may buy gluten free porridge oats in most large supermarkets for children who have a gluten allergy.
Macaroni Cheese	You may buy gluten free pasta in most large supermarkets for children who have a gluten allergy. Lactose free margarine, hard cheese and milk (eg soy or rice milk) may be used for children who are lactose intolerant.
Vegetable Samosas	This recipe is not suitable for children with gluten/wheat allergies.

Lightning Source UK Ltd.
Milton Keynes UK
UKOW07f2144301115

263690UK00005B/23/P